Email Marketing Mastery: A Hands-On Approach for Small Business Owners

Tyler Ryan

Published by Tyler Ryan, 2023.

While every precaution has been taken in the preparation of this book, the publisher assumes no responsibility for errors or omissions, or for damages resulting from the use of the information contained herein.

EMAIL MARKETING MASTERY: A HANDS-ON APPROACH FOR SMALL BUSINESS OWNERS

First edition. September 6, 2023.

ISBN: 979-8223870142

Written by Tyler Ryan.

Table of Contents

Chapter 1: Introduction to Email Marketing

Understanding the Power of Email Marketing

In today's digital age, email marketing has emerged as one of the most powerful tools for small businesses to connect with their target audience and drive sales. With its ability to reach customers directly in their inbox, email marketing offers a unique opportunity to build relationships, increase brand awareness, and generate valuable leads. In this subchapter, we will delve into the various aspects of email marketing and how it can revolutionize your small business.

First and foremost, we will explore the importance of building an email list. As a small business owner, your email list is your most valuable asset. It consists of individuals who have willingly shared their contact information and expressed interest in your products or services. We will discuss effective strategies to grow your email list organically, ensuring that you reach the right audience and avoid spamming.

Next, we will dive into the art of crafting compelling email content. A well-crafted email can grab the attention of your recipients, engage them with valuable information, and motivate them to take action. We will provide practical tips and examples to help you create attention-grabbing subject lines, personalized content, and effective calls-to-action. Whether you are sending promotional emails, newsletters, or automated sequences, mastering the art of email content is crucial for success.

Furthermore, we will explore the power of segmentation and personalization in email marketing. By dividing your email list into specific segments based on demographics, interests, or purchase history, you can tailor your messages to resonate with each group. We will discuss how to leverage customer data and analytics to deliver personalized content that speaks directly to your audience's needs and desires.

Additionally, we will delve into the world of automation and email marketing tools. Small business owners often have limited time and resources, making automation a game-changer. We will introduce you to various automation tools that can streamline your email marketing efforts, from welcome emails and drip campaigns to abandoned cart reminders and customer follow-ups.

Lastly, we will touch upon email deliverability and compliance. Understanding the technical aspects of email marketing, such as email authentication and best practices for avoiding spam filters, is essential to ensure that your emails reach the intended recipients and comply with legal regulations.

By the end of this subchapter, you will have a comprehensive understanding of the power of email marketing and how it can benefit your small business. Armed with the knowledge and practical tips provided, you will be ready to implement effective email marketing strategies that can drive growth, engage customers, and boost your bottom line.

Benefits of Email Marketing for Small Businesses

In today's digital age, email marketing has emerged as a powerful tool for small businesses to connect with customers and drive growth. In this subchapter, we will explore the numerous benefits that email marketing brings to small businesses, helping them build brand loyalty, increase sales, and achieve long-term success.

First and foremost, email marketing is incredibly cost-effective, making it an ideal choice for small businesses with limited budgets. Unlike traditional marketing channels, such as print media or television ads, email marketing allows you to reach a large audience at a fraction of the cost. With affordable email marketing platforms readily available, small businesses can create and send professional-looking emails without breaking the bank.

Another significant advantage of email marketing is its ability to reach a targeted audience. By building an email list of interested customers and prospects, small businesses can tailor their messages to specific segments, ensuring that the right content is delivered to the right people at the right time. This targeted approach not only increases the likelihood of conversion but also enhances customer satisfaction by providing relevant and personalized information.

Moreover, email marketing offers a high return on investment (ROI). With the ability to track open rates, click-through rates, and conversion rates, small businesses can analyze the effectiveness of their email campaigns and make data-driven improvements. This level of measurability allows for continuous optimization, resulting in higher ROI and improved overall marketing strategies.

Furthermore, email marketing enables small businesses to build strong relationships with their customers. By regularly sending valuable and engaging content, businesses can establish trust and credibility, positioning themselves as industry experts and thought leaders. Through email newsletters, businesses can share useful tips, industry news, and exclusive offers, fostering a sense of loyalty and encouraging repeat purchases.

Lastly, email marketing provides a platform for small businesses to communicate directly with their customers. Unlike social media or search engine advertising, which can be subject to algorithms or other external factors, emails land directly in the recipient's inbox, ensuring maximum visibility. This direct line of communication allows businesses to promptly address customer concerns, gather feedback, and keep customers informed about new products or services.

In conclusion, email marketing offers a myriad of benefits for small businesses. From cost-effectiveness and targeted reach to high ROI and customer relationship building, email marketing serves as a powerful tool for small business owners to drive growth and achieve long-term success. By mastering the art of email marketing, small businesses can stay competitive in today's digital landscape and take their businesses to new heights.

Common Mistakes to Avoid in Email Marketing

Subchapter: Common Mistakes to Avoid in Email Marketing
Introduction:
In the competitive world of digital marketing, email marketing continues to be a powerful tool for small businesses to engage with their target audience and drive sales. However, many small business owners make common mistakes that can hinder the success of their email marketing campaigns. This subchapter aims to highlight these mistakes and provide practical tips for small business owners to avoid them, ensuring their email marketing efforts yield the desired results.
1. Neglecting to Build a Targeted Email List:

One of the biggest mistakes small business owners make is sending emails to a broad audience without considering their interests or preferences. Instead, focus on building a targeted email list by segmenting your subscribers based on their demographics, purchase history, or engagement levels. This way, you can send personalized and relevant content, increasing open rates and conversions.

2. Failing to Craft Compelling Subject Lines:

Your subject line is the gatekeeper to your email. Avoid generic or spammy subject lines that may be flagged or ignored by recipients. Craft concise, attention-grabbing subject lines that pique curiosity and create a sense of urgency. A well-crafted subject line improves open rates and encourages recipients to engage with your email content.

3. Overwhelming Subscribers with Excessive Emails:

Bombarding your subscribers with too many emails can lead to annoyance and unsubscribes. Find the right balance by planning your email frequency and ensuring each email provides value. Quality over quantity is key. Create a content calendar and send emails at regular intervals to maintain engagement without overwhelming your subscribers.

4. Neglecting Mobile Optimization:

With the increasing use of smartphones, it's crucial to optimize your emails for mobile devices. Neglecting mobile optimization can result in poor user experience and lower conversion rates. Ensure your emails are responsive, load quickly, and have a mobile-friendly layout to capture the attention of your mobile audience.

5. Ignoring Email Analytics:

Failing to track and analyze email metrics is a missed opportunity for improvement. Pay attention to open rates, click-through rates, conversion rates, and other key metrics. Analyzing this data can help you refine your email marketing strategy, identify what works, and make necessary adjustments to optimize your campaigns.

Conclusion:

Avoiding these common mistakes can significantly improve your email marketing efforts as a small business owner. By building a targeted email list, crafting compelling subject lines, finding the right email frequency, optimizing for mobile devices, and analyzing email metrics, you can enhance engagement, drive conversions, and build lasting relationships with your subscribers. Embrace these best practices to master the art of email marketing and propel your small business to new heights.

Chapter 2: Building a Strong Foundation

Defining Your Email Marketing Goals

For small business owners, email marketing can be a powerful tool to engage with customers, build brand loyalty, and drive sales. However, without clear goals in mind, your email marketing efforts may lack direction and fail to deliver the desired results. In this subchapter, we will explore the importance of defining your email marketing goals and how to set objectives that align with your small business.

Why Define Your Email Marketing Goals?

Defining your email marketing goals is crucial for several reasons. Firstly, it helps you establish a clear vision of what you want to achieve through your email campaigns. Whether it's increasing website traffic, boosting sales, or building a loyal customer base, having a well-defined goal allows you to tailor your strategies and measure your success.

Secondly, setting goals helps you prioritize your efforts and allocate resources effectively. With limited time and budget, you can focus on activities that directly contribute to achieving your objectives. By understanding your goals, you can make informed decisions about email content, segmentation, and automation, ensuring that your efforts are optimized for maximum impact.

Setting SMART Goals

To effectively define your email marketing goals, it is essential to follow the SMART framework – Specific, Measurable, Attainable, Relevant, and Time-bound. Specific goals are clear and concise, leaving no room for ambiguity. Measurable goals allow you to track progress and evaluate success. Attainable goals are realistic and achievable based on your resources and capabilities. Relevant goals align with your overall business objectives and target audience. Lastly, time-bound goals have a set deadline, creating a sense of urgency and providing a timeframe for evaluation.

Examples of Email Marketing Goals

Here are a few examples of email marketing goals that small business owners can consider:

1. Increase website traffic by 20% through email campaigns within six months.

2. Generate a 15% increase in online sales through targeted email promotions over the next quarter.

3. Build a loyal customer base by increasing email subscribers by 30% within one year.

4. Improve customer engagement by achieving a 10% increase in email open rates within three months.

5. Enhance brand awareness by obtaining a 25% click-through rate on email newsletters within six months.

Remember, these goals should be tailored to your specific business needs and objectives. By defining your email marketing goals, you can create a roadmap for success and take full advantage of this powerful marketing channel for your small business.

Identifying Your Target Audience

In the world of email marketing for small businesses, one of the most critical factors for success is identifying your target audience. Knowing who your ideal customers are and understanding their needs and preferences is essential in crafting effective email marketing campaigns that drive engagement and conversions. In this subchapter, we will delve into the process of identifying your target audience and provide practical strategies to help you reach and resonate with them.

The first step in identifying your target audience is conducting thorough market research. This involves analyzing demographic data, such as age, gender, location, and income level, to gain insights into who your potential customers are. Additionally, psychographic factors, such as their interests, values, and lifestyle choices, can provide valuable information about their motivations and purchasing behaviors.

Once you have gathered relevant data, it's time to create buyer personas. Buyer personas are fictional representations of your ideal customers, based on the information you have gathered. These personas help you humanize your target audience and make it easier to tailor your email marketing messages to their specific needs and interests. We will discuss the process of creating buyer personas in detail, including examples and templates to guide you through the process.

Furthermore, understanding your target audience's pain points and challenges is crucial in developing email content that resonates with them. By addressing their specific problems and offering relevant solutions, you can position yourself as a trusted advisor and build meaningful connections with your subscribers. We will explore various techniques to gather insights about your audience's pain points and discuss how to leverage that information to create compelling email campaigns.

Additionally, we will explore the importance of segmenting your email list based on your target audience's characteristics. By dividing your subscribers into smaller, more targeted groups, you can deliver more personalized and relevant content. We will discuss different segmentation strategies and provide step-by-step instructions on how to implement them effectively.

In conclusion, identifying your target audience is the foundation of successful email marketing for small businesses. By conducting thorough market research, creating buyer personas, understanding pain points, and implementing effective segmentation strategies, you can craft email campaigns that resonate with your audience and drive tangible results for your business. This subchapter will equip you with the knowledge and tools to identify and connect with your target audience, ultimately helping you achieve email marketing mastery for your small business.

Creating a Compelling Value Proposition

In the fast-paced world of email marketing for small businesses, having a compelling value proposition is essential to stand out from the competition and attract customers. A value proposition is a statement that clearly communicates the unique benefits and value that your product or service offers to customers. It is the foundation upon which your entire email marketing strategy is built, allowing you to engage with your target audience and drive conversions.

The first step in creating a compelling value proposition is to understand your target audience. As a small business owner, you need to identify the specific needs, challenges, and desires of your customers. Conduct thorough market research, analyze customer data, and listen to feedback to gain insights into what your audience truly values. By understanding their pain points and aspirations, you can tailor your value proposition to address their needs effectively.

Once you have a clear understanding of your target audience, it's time to craft a value proposition that sets your small business apart. Start by highlighting the unique features or benefits of your product or service that directly solve your customers' problems. Focus on the outcomes and results they can expect by choosing your business over others. Use clear and concise language to convey your message, avoiding jargon or technical terms that might confuse or alienate your audience.

To make your value proposition even more compelling, consider adding a touch of emotion. Small business owners often have a personal story or mission behind their venture, and incorporating this into your value proposition can create a stronger connection with customers. Share your passion, values, or the journey that led you to start your business, emphasizing how it aligns with the needs and desires of your target audience.

Once your value proposition is crafted, it's time to integrate it into your email marketing campaigns. Every email you send should reinforce your value proposition, whether it's through the subject line, the email copy, or the call-to-action. Consistency is key to building trust and credibility with your audience.

In conclusion, creating a compelling value proposition is crucial for small business owners in the realm of email marketing. By understanding your target audience, highlighting unique features, and incorporating emotion, you can craft a value proposition that resonates with your customers. Integrate it into your email marketing campaigns consistently to engage your audience and drive conversions. Remember, a strong value proposition is the key to standing out and succeeding in the competitive world of email marketing for small businesses.

Chapter 3: Building an Effective Email List

Implementing Opt-In Forms on Your Website

As a small business owner, you understand the importance of email marketing for growing your customer base and increasing sales. One of the most effective ways to build your email list is by implementing opt-in forms on your website. In this subchapter, we will delve into the various strategies and best practices for incorporating opt-in forms seamlessly into your website.

Opt-in forms are a powerful tool that allows you to collect email addresses from visitors who have willingly chosen to receive updates and promotions from your business. By adding these forms strategically to your website, you can capture valuable leads and nurture them into loyal customers.

To begin, you need to consider the placement of your opt-in forms. It is essential to position them in prominent areas where visitors are likely to notice them. You could experiment with placing them on the sidebar, in the header or footer, or even as a pop-up that appears after a certain period of time or when a visitor is about to exit your site. A/B testing can help you determine the most effective placement for your specific audience.

The design and messaging of your opt-in forms also play a crucial role in their success. It is important to keep the design clean, visually appealing, and consistent with your brand. The copy should be concise, compelling, and offer a clear benefit to the subscriber. Remember to include a strong call-to-action that encourages visitors to sign up. Offering incentives, such as exclusive discounts or access to valuable content, can significantly boost opt-in rates.

Once you have captured email addresses, it is vital to respect your subscribers' privacy and adhere to email marketing best practices. Ensure that you have a clear privacy policy in place, and always obtain explicit permission from subscribers to send them marketing emails. Implementing a double opt-in process adds an extra layer of confirmation, reducing the chances of spam complaints and improving the quality of your email list.

Regularly analyzing and optimizing your opt-in forms is key to maximizing their effectiveness. Monitor metrics such as conversion rates, bounce rates, and engagement levels to identify areas for improvement. Experiment with different form styles, colors, and copy to see what resonates best with your audience.

By implementing opt-in forms on your website and following these best practices, you can build a strong and engaged email list that will drive growth for your small business. Remember, email marketing is a long-term strategy, and nurturing relationships with your subscribers will lead to increased brand loyalty and higher conversion rates.

Using Lead Magnets to Grow Your Email List

In the ever-evolving world of email marketing for small businesses, building a robust and engaged email list is crucial for success. One of the most effective strategies to accomplish this is by using lead magnets. Lead magnets are valuable resources or incentives that you offer to your target audience in exchange for their email addresses. These can be in the form of e-books, whitepapers, checklists, templates, webinars, or exclusive discounts.

Why are lead magnets so powerful? By offering something of value, you entice potential customers to willingly share their contact information, giving you permission to communicate with them directly. This allows you to nurture these leads, build trust, and eventually convert them into loyal customers. Here are some key strategies to effectively use lead magnets to grow your email list.

Firstly, it's essential to understand your target audience and what they find valuable. Conduct thorough market research to identify their pain points, needs, and desires. This will help you create lead magnets that directly address their specific challenges, making them more likely to opt in and become subscribers.

Next, optimize your website and landing pages to capture leads effectively. Create compelling call-to-action buttons, strategically place lead capture forms, and ensure that your landing pages are visually appealing and easy to navigate. Make sure the process of opting in is simple and hassle-free to encourage more sign-ups.

Promotion is key. Develop a multi-channel marketing strategy to promote your lead magnets and capture leads from various sources. Leverage social media platforms, content marketing, paid advertising, and partnerships to reach a wider audience. Use enticing headlines and persuasive copy to compel your target audience to take action and sign up for your lead magnets.

Once you have built your email list, nurture your subscribers by delivering valuable and relevant content. Provide them with exclusive insights, tips, and advice related to their interests. Personalize your emails to make your subscribers feel valued and understood. This will increase engagement and the likelihood of them becoming long-term customers.

Lastly, continuously analyze and optimize your lead generation efforts. Monitor the performance of your lead magnets, landing pages, and email campaigns. Test different variations to determine what works best for your audience. Collect feedback from your subscribers to gauge their satisfaction and make necessary improvements.

In conclusion, using lead magnets is a powerful strategy to grow your email list and drive business growth. By offering valuable resources and incentives, you attract potential customers and establish a direct line of communication. With careful planning, promotion, and nurturing, you can convert these leads into loyal customers, ultimately boosting your small business's success.

Strategies for Capturing Email Addresses Offline

As a small business owner, you understand the importance of email marketing in building and maintaining relationships with your customers. While online methods of capturing email addresses are effective, there are also numerous opportunities offline that you can leverage to grow your email list. In this subchapter, we will explore some strategies for capturing email addresses offline and how they can benefit your small business.

1. In-store Sign-up Forms: Make it easy for customers to provide their email addresses by placing sign-up forms at strategic locations in your store. Offer an incentive, such as a discount or exclusive content, to encourage customers to sign up.

2. Paper Sign-up Sheets: For businesses that attend events, trade shows, or networking functions, having a paper sign-up sheet can be an effective way to collect email addresses. Ensure that the sheet is easily visible and include a brief description of the benefits customers will receive by subscribing to your email list.

3. Business Cards: When interacting with potential customers, always carry business cards that include a call-to-action to join your email list. Consider offering a special bonus or resource to entice recipients to sign up.

4. Invoices and Receipts: Include a call-to-action on your invoices and receipts, encouraging customers to subscribe to your email list. Make it clear how being on the list will benefit them, such as receiving exclusive discounts or updates on new products.

5. Contests and Giveaways: Host contests or giveaways at your store or during events, where participants must provide their email addresses to enter. This strategy not only builds your email list but also generates excitement and engagement among your target audience.

6. Direct Mail: If your business utilizes direct mail marketing, include a call-to-action on your mailers, inviting recipients to subscribe to your email list. Mention the benefits they will receive, such as access to special promotions or insider information.

Remember, when collecting email addresses offline, it is crucial to inform customers about how their information will be used and assure them of their privacy. Clearly communicate the value they will receive by being on your email list, and always provide an easy opt-out option.

By implementing these strategies for capturing email addresses offline, you can significantly grow your email list and enhance your email marketing efforts. Building a strong email list will allow you to stay connected with your customers, provide valuable content, and ultimately increase sales and customer loyalty.

Chapter 4: Crafting Engaging Email Content

Writing Attention-Grabbing Subject Lines

In the world of email marketing for small businesses, one of the most crucial elements that can make or break your campaign is the subject line. Your subject line is the first thing your recipients see in their inbox, and it plays a vital role in determining whether they will open your email or simply ignore it. Crafting attention-grabbing subject lines is a skill that every small business owner should master to increase open rates and ultimately drive more conversions.

1. Keep it concise and compelling: Small business owners often have limited time to grab their readers' attention. Therefore, it is essential to keep your subject lines concise and compelling. Aim for a maximum of 50 characters to ensure that your message is clear and easy to understand at a glance.

2. Personalize whenever possible: Personalization is a powerful tool in email marketing. Addressing your recipients by their names or tailoring the subject line to their specific needs and interests can significantly increase open rates. Take advantage of the data you have about your subscribers to create personalized subject lines that resonate with them.

3. Create a sense of urgency: People are more likely to act when there is a sense of urgency involved. Incorporating words like "limited time offer," "exclusive deal," or "ending soon" in your subject lines can create a sense of urgency and entice your recipients to open your email right away.

4. Use numbers and statistics: Numbers and statistics have a way of capturing attention. Including specific numbers or statistics in your subject lines can pique curiosity and make your email seem more tangible and credible. For example, "Increase your website traffic by 50% with our proven strategies" is more compelling than a generic subject line like "Boost your website traffic."

5. A/B test your subject lines: Every audience is different, and what works for one may not work for another. A/B testing is a valuable technique to determine which subject lines resonate the most with your specific audience. Split your email list into two segments and send different subject lines to each group.

Analyze the open rates to identify which subject line performs better and refine your approach accordingly.

Remember, the subject line is the gateway to your email content. By mastering the art of writing attention-grabbing subject lines, small business owners can significantly improve their email marketing campaigns, increase open rates, and ultimately drive more conversions. So, take the time to craft compelling subject lines that speak to your audience and watch your email marketing efforts thrive.

Creating Compelling Email Copy

In today's digital age, email marketing has become an indispensable tool for small businesses to connect with their customers and drive sales. However, with inboxes flooded with countless emails every day, it is crucial for small business owners to create compelling email copy that stands out from the crowd. This subchapter will guide you through the process of crafting effective and engaging email content that captures your audience's attention and drives them to take action.

1. Understanding Your Audience:

Before diving into creating email copy, it is essential to know your audience intimately. What are their pain points, desires, and aspirations? Tailor your email content to address these specific needs, ensuring that your message resonates with your target audience.

2. Crafting Attention-Grabbing Subject Lines:

The subject line of your email is the first thing that recipients see in their inbox. It should be concise, compelling, and enticing enough to make them want to open the email. Use strong action words, personalization, or intriguing questions to pique their curiosity and increase open rates.

3. Personalization:

Make your emails feel personalized and relevant to each recipient. Address them by their name and segment your email list based on their preferences, purchase history, or demographics. Personalized emails have higher engagement rates and make your audience feel valued.

4. Writing Engaging Body Copy:

Keep your email content concise, clear, and to the point. Use a conversational tone that resonates with your audience. Highlight the benefits of your products or services, and focus on how they can solve their problems. Incorporate storytelling techniques to make your email more relatable and engaging.

5. Call-to-Action:

Every email should have a clear and compelling call-to-action (CTA). Whether it's directing the reader to make a purchase, sign up for a webinar, or download an ebook, make sure the CTA is persuasive and easy to follow. Use action verbs and create a sense of urgency to prompt immediate action.

6. A/B Testing:

To optimize your email copy, conduct A/B testing by sending different versions of your email to a small sample of your audience. Test different subject lines, body copy variations, CTAs, and even visuals. Analyze the results and identify which version performs better before sending it to your entire email list.

Remember, consistency is key in email marketing. Regularly provide valuable content, nurture your relationship with your audience, and always strive to improve your email copy based on their feedback and response. With compelling email copy, you can engage your small business audience and drive them towards success.

Incorporating Visual Elements in Your Emails

In today's digital age, email marketing has become an essential tool for small businesses to connect with their target audience and drive conversions. With the increasing competition in the online space, it is crucial for small business owners to stand out from the crowd. One effective way to achieve this is by incorporating visual elements in your emails.

Visual elements, such as images, videos, infographics, and gifs, can significantly enhance the overall appeal and impact of your emails. They catch the reader's attention and make your message more engaging and memorable. By leveraging the power of visuals, you can effectively convey your brand's personality, showcase your products or services, and create a lasting impression on your subscribers.

When using visual elements in your emails, it is essential to keep a few key things in mind. Firstly, make sure that the visuals you choose align with your brand's identity and messaging. Consistency is key in establishing a strong brand image, so ensure that your visuals are in line with your logo, color scheme, and overall design.

Secondly, optimize your visual elements for different devices and email clients. With the increasing use of mobile devices, it is crucial to ensure that your visuals are responsive and load quickly on smartphones and tablets. Test your emails across various devices and platforms to ensure a seamless user experience.

Furthermore, the placement of visual elements in your emails is also crucial. Use eye-catching visuals strategically to guide the reader's attention towards your call-to-action (CTA) or important information. A well-placed image or video can significantly increase click-through rates and conversions.

However, it is important to strike a balance between text and visuals in your emails. While visuals are powerful, excessive use of graphics can lead to longer loading times and potential deliverability issues. Remember that some email clients may block images by default, so always include alt text to provide context and ensure your message is conveyed even without the visuals.

Lastly, regularly analyze the performance of your visual elements. Monitor open rates, click-through rates, and conversions to understand what visuals resonate best with your audience. A/B testing different visuals can help you refine your email marketing strategy and continually improve your results.

Incorporating visual elements in your emails is a powerful way to engage your audience, enhance your brand's image, and drive conversions. By carefully selecting and strategically placing visuals, optimizing for different devices, and analyzing performance, small business owners can take their email marketing efforts to new heights. So, don't be afraid to get creative and make your emails visually appealing to leave a lasting impression on your subscribers.

Chapter 5: Designing Eye-Catching Email Templates

Understanding the Importance of Email Design

In today's digital age, email marketing has become an essential tool for small businesses to engage with their audience, build brand awareness, and drive conversions. However, simply sending out emails is not enough to achieve success in this competitive landscape. The design of your emails plays a crucial role in catching the attention of your recipients and conveying your message effectively. In this subchapter, we will delve into the importance of email design and how it can significantly impact the success of your email marketing campaigns.

First and foremost, well-designed emails can create a positive first impression and establish credibility for your brand. When recipients open an email that looks outdated, cluttered, or unprofessional, they are more likely to disregard the message or mark it as spam. On the other hand, a visually appealing email with a clean layout, eye-catching graphics, and cohesive branding elements immediately grabs attention and encourages recipients to engage with the content.

Moreover, email design plays a crucial role in enhancing the readability and comprehension of your message. By utilizing clear and concise copy, strategically placed headlines, and relevant imagery, you can ensure that your recipients quickly grasp the purpose of your email. In addition, an effective design can guide readers through the email, leading them to important calls-to-action and ultimately driving conversions.

Furthermore, with the increasing number of people accessing emails on mobile devices, responsive email design has become imperative. A well-designed email should automatically adapt to different screen sizes, ensuring a seamless user experience across various devices. By neglecting responsive design, you risk frustrating your recipients with emails that are difficult to read or navigate on mobile devices, leading to a significant loss in engagement and conversions.

Ultimately, investing time and effort into email design is crucial for small business owners looking to maximize the effectiveness of their email marketing campaigns. Whether it's crafting visually appealing templates, optimizing for mobile devices, or personalizing the design to match your brand's identity, each element contributes to the overall success of your emails.

In the following chapters, we will explore best practices for email design, including how to choose the right color palette, select engaging imagery, and optimize your layout for maximum impact. By mastering the art of email design, you will be able to create compelling emails that stand out in crowded inboxes, resonate with your audience, and drive the desired results for your small business.

Choosing the Right Email Template

When it comes to email marketing for small businesses, one of the most important factors in achieving success is choosing the right email template. An email template is essentially a pre-designed layout that allows you to create professional-looking emails without the need for extensive design skills or coding knowledge. It provides a framework for your content and ensures that your message is delivered in a visually appealing and cohesive manner.

There are numerous email templates available, and selecting the right one can make a significant difference in the effectiveness of your email campaigns. Here are a few key considerations to keep in mind when choosing the right email template for your small business:

1. Consider your brand identity: Your email template should align with your brand identity and reflect the overall look and feel of your business. Choose a template that incorporates your brand colors, fonts, and logo to reinforce brand recognition and consistency.

2. Mobile responsiveness: With an increasing number of people accessing emails on their mobile devices, it is crucial to choose a template that is mobile responsive. This ensures that your emails will display correctly across different screen sizes and devices, providing a seamless experience for your recipients.

3. Customizability: Look for templates that offer customization options, allowing you to tailor the layout, colors, and content to suit your specific needs. This flexibility enables you to create unique and engaging email campaigns that resonate with your target audience.

4. Clear call-to-action: A well-designed email template should emphasize your call-to-action (CTA) and make it easily identifiable. Whether it's a button or a text link, the CTA should stand out and prompt recipients to take the

desired action, such as making a purchase, signing up for a newsletter, or visiting your website.

5. Testing and analytics: Opt for an email template that integrates with email marketing platforms that provide testing and analytics capabilities. This allows you to track the performance of your emails, analyze metrics such as open rates and click-through rates, and make data-driven decisions to optimize your campaigns.

By carefully considering these factors and choosing the right email template, you can create compelling and visually appealing emails that drive engagement, conversions, and ultimately, business growth. Remember that email marketing is a powerful tool for small businesses, and investing time and effort into selecting the right email template is a crucial step towards achieving success in your email marketing campaigns.

Customizing Email Templates to Match Your Brand

In today's competitive business landscape, it is more important than ever for small businesses to stand out from the crowd and establish a unique brand identity. One powerful tool that can help you achieve this is email marketing. By leveraging the potential of email marketing, small business owners can effectively reach out to their target audience, build brand loyalty, and drive sales.

However, simply sending out generic emails won't cut it. To make a lasting impression, you need to customize your email templates to match your brand. This subchapter will guide you through the process of creating personalized email templates that align with your brand identity.

First and foremost, it is crucial to have a clear understanding of your brand. Define your unique selling proposition, brand voice, and key visual elements such as your logo, color palette, and typography. These elements should be consistent across all your marketing channels, including your email templates.

Once you have a solid grasp of your brand identity, it's time to start customizing your email templates. Most email marketing platforms offer a wide range of pre-designed templates that you can choose from. While these templates are convenient, they may not reflect your brand's personality. To truly stand out, consider working with a professional designer to create custom templates that accurately represent your brand.

When customizing your email templates, pay attention to the following elements:

1. Logo and branding: Incorporate your logo and brand colors into the email header and footer to reinforce brand recognition.

2. Typography: Choose fonts that align with your brand's personality. Use a legible font for the body text and a bolder font for headings and call-to-action buttons.

3. Color scheme: Select colors that complement your brand palette, ensuring consistency with your website and other marketing materials.

4. Images: Include high-quality images that resonate with your brand and product offerings. Avoid generic stock photos and opt for custom visuals whenever possible.

5. Personalization: Tailor your email content to address your audience by their names, making them feel valued and connected to your brand.

By customizing your email templates to match your brand, you can create a cohesive and memorable experience for your subscribers. Consistency across all touchpoints will strengthen your brand identity and help build trust with your audience. Remember, in the world of email marketing for small businesses, brand differentiation is key to success.

Chapter 6: Automating Your Email Marketing

Introduction to Email Marketing Automation

Email marketing is a powerful tool for small businesses to connect with their target audience, build relationships, and drive sales. However, as a small business owner, you are likely juggling multiple responsibilities and may not have the time or resources to manually send individual emails to each subscriber on your list. This is where email marketing automation comes in.

In this subchapter, we will explore the concept of email marketing automation and how it can benefit your small business. We will discuss the various automation tools available and provide practical tips on how to implement automation strategies effectively.

Email marketing automation involves using software to automate various tasks in your email marketing campaigns. This can include sending welcome emails to new subscribers, segmenting your list based on specific criteria, sending personalized content based on customer behavior, and even re-engaging inactive subscribers.

One of the key benefits of email marketing automation is that it saves you time and effort. By automating repetitive tasks, you can focus on other important aspects of your business while still maintaining a consistent and engaging email marketing strategy.

Furthermore, automation allows you to deliver highly targeted and personalized content to your subscribers. By segmenting your list based on demographics, interests, or previous interactions, you can tailor your emails to resonate with each individual recipient. This level of personalization not only increases engagement but also improves the chances of converting subscribers into customers.

In this subchapter, we will guide you through the process of setting up email marketing automation for your small business. We will cover topics such as choosing the right automation software, understanding the different automation features, and creating effective automated email sequences.

Whether you are new to email marketing or looking to take your current strategy to the next level, this subchapter will provide you with the knowledge and tools you need to succeed. By harnessing the power of email marketing automation, you can streamline your campaigns, connect with your audience on a deeper level, and ultimately drive the growth of your small business.

Continue reading to discover the endless possibilities that email marketing automation can offer for your small business.

Setting Up Automated Welcome Emails

Welcome emails are an essential part of any email marketing campaign. They provide an opportunity to make a positive first impression on your subscribers, establish a connection, and set the stage for building a long-term relationship. However, manually sending welcome emails to each new subscriber can be time-consuming and inefficient. That's where automated welcome emails come in.

In this subchapter, we will delve into the process of setting up automated welcome emails, specifically tailored for small business owners looking to leverage the power of email marketing.

The first step in setting up automated welcome emails is choosing the right email marketing platform. There are several options available, each with its own set of features and pricing plans. We will explore popular platforms that are user-friendly, cost-effective, and cater specifically to the needs of small businesses.

Once you have selected an email marketing platform, we will guide you through the process of creating an effective welcome email series. We will discuss the key components of a welcome email, including a warm greeting, a brief introduction to your business, and a clear call-to-action. We will also provide examples and templates to help you craft compelling welcome emails that resonate with your target audience.

Next, we will show you how to automate the delivery of welcome emails. This involves setting up triggers based on specific actions, such as subscribing to your newsletter or making a purchase. We will explain how to integrate your email marketing platform with your website or e-commerce platform to ensure seamless automation.

Furthermore, we will explore the importance of personalization in welcome emails. Small business owners can leverage customer data to create personalized experiences for their subscribers. We will discuss strategies for segmenting your audience and tailoring welcome emails accordingly, leading to higher engagement and conversion rates.

Finally, we will provide tips and best practices for optimizing your automated welcome email series. From testing different subject lines and email content to analyzing metrics and making necessary adjustments, we will equip you with the tools to continuously improve your email marketing efforts.

By the end of this subchapter, you will have the knowledge and skills to set up an automated welcome email series that engages your subscribers, builds trust, and drives business growth. With email marketing being a cost-effective and powerful tool for small businesses, mastering the art of automated welcome emails is an essential step towards achieving marketing success.

Implementing Drip Campaigns to Nurture Leads

In today's digital age, email marketing has become an indispensable tool for small businesses. It provides a cost-effective and efficient way to reach a wide audience, build relationships, and ultimately, drive sales. However, simply sending out sporadic emails to your subscribers is not enough to maximize the potential of your email marketing efforts. This is where drip campaigns come into play.

Drip campaigns, also known as automated email campaigns, are a series of pre-scheduled emails that are sent out to your subscribers over a specified period. The goal is to nurture leads, guide them through the buyer's journey, and increase the chances of conversion. By implementing drip campaigns, small business owners can ensure that their email marketing efforts are consistent, targeted, and personalized.

The first step in implementing drip campaigns is to define your goals and segment your subscriber list. Identify the different stages of the buyer's journey and create content tailored specifically for each stage. For instance, a prospect who has just subscribed to your newsletter may receive a welcome email followed by a series of educational emails to build trust and provide value. On the other hand, a lead who has shown interest in a specific product or service may receive a series of promotional emails highlighting its features, benefits, and testimonials.

Once you have segmented your list and created relevant content, it's time to set up your automation software. There are numerous email marketing platforms available that offer easy-to-use drip campaign functionality. These platforms allow you to schedule and automate the delivery of your emails based on triggers or time intervals. You can also track and analyze the performance of your drip campaigns to identify areas of improvement and optimize your strategy.

One of the key advantages of drip campaigns is their ability to provide a personalized experience for your subscribers. By leveraging data and insights from your email marketing platform, you can customize the content, timing, and frequency of your emails based on individual preferences and behavior. This level of personalization not only increases engagement but also fosters a stronger connection with your audience.

In conclusion, implementing drip campaigns in your email marketing strategy can significantly enhance your ability to nurture leads and drive conversions. By segmenting your subscriber list, creating relevant content, and leveraging automation software, small business owners can deliver targeted and personalized emails that guide prospects through the buyer's journey. Take advantage of the power of drip campaigns and watch your email marketing efforts flourish.

Chapter 7: Effective Email Campaign Strategies

Segmenting Your Email List for Targeted Campaigns

In today's competitive business landscape, email marketing has become an essential tool for small businesses to reach and engage their target audience. However, sending out generic emails to your entire subscriber list may not yield the desired results. To truly maximize the potential of your email campaigns, it is crucial to segment your email list and tailor your messages to specific groups within your audience. This subchapter will guide you on how to effectively segment your email list for targeted campaigns, helping you achieve better open rates, click-through rates, and ultimately, higher conversions.

Segmentation is the process of dividing your email list into smaller, more targeted groups based on various criteria such as demographics, interests, purchase history, or engagement levels. By doing so, you can craft personalized messages that resonate with each segment, increasing the likelihood of capturing their attention and driving them to take action.

To begin segmenting your email list, start by analyzing your subscriber data. Look for commonalities and patterns that can help you categorize your audience into distinct groups. For example, you may have a segment of loyal customers who have made multiple purchases, a segment of potential customers who have signed up for your newsletter but haven't made a purchase yet, or a segment of customers who have shown interest in a particular product or service.

Once you have identified your segments, it's time to create targeted campaigns that speak directly to each group's needs and interests. Tailor your email content, subject lines, and call-to-actions to resonate with each segment, making them feel like you understand their specific pain points and can provide the solutions they are seeking. Personalization is key here, as it helps build trust and credibility with your audience.

Segmentation also allows you to send targeted offers and promotions to specific segments, increasing the chances of converting leads into customers. For example, you can offer a special discount to your loyal customers as a token of appreciation for their continued support or send a series of nurturing emails to your potential customers to guide them through the buying process.

In conclusion, segmenting your email list for targeted campaigns is an essential strategy for small business owners looking to maximize the effectiveness of their email marketing efforts. By understanding your audience and tailoring your messages to specific segments, you can increase engagement, build stronger relationships, and ultimately drive more conversions. So, take the time to analyze your subscriber data, identify your segments, and start crafting personalized email campaigns that will resonate with your audience and help your small business thrive.

Personalizing Emails for Better Engagement

In the world of email marketing for small businesses, personalization is the key to boosting engagement and building meaningful connections with your audience. Gone are the days of generic, one-size-fits-all email campaigns. Today, customers expect personalized content that speaks directly to their needs and interests. In this subchapter, we will explore the power of personalization and how it can transform your email marketing strategy.

First and foremost, personalizing your emails shows your audience that you value their individuality. By addressing recipients by their names and tailoring the content to their preferences, you create a sense of familiarity and trust. Studies have shown that personalized emails have higher open rates, click-through rates, and conversion rates compared to their non-personalized counterparts.

To begin personalizing your email campaigns, start by collecting relevant data from your subscribers. This can include their names, locations, purchase history, and browsing behavior. By leveraging this information, you can segment your email list and send targeted messages to specific groups of subscribers. For example, if you own a clothing store and your data shows that a group of customers frequently purchases men's shoes, you can send them personalized offers or product recommendations tailored to their interests.

Another effective personalization technique is dynamic content. With the help of marketing automation tools, you can dynamically change the content of your emails based on specific criteria. For instance, you can showcase different products to different segments of your audience, or even change the entire email layout based on their demographics or past interactions with your brand.

Beyond basic personalization, it's crucial to craft compelling subject lines that grab attention and entice your recipients to open your emails. Use their first names or reference their recent purchases to make the subject lines feel more personalized and relevant. Additionally, experiment with different email copy and design elements to find the most engaging combination for your audience. A/B testing can help you identify the strategies that resonate best with your subscribers.

In conclusion, personalizing your emails is the key to boosting engagement and driving better results for your small business. By leveraging customer data, segmenting your audience, and using dynamic content, you can deliver tailored messages that resonate with your subscribers. Remember, personalization goes beyond just addressing recipients by name; it's about delivering relevant and meaningful content that connects with your audience on a personal level. Implement these strategies in your email marketing efforts, and watch your engagement metrics soar.

A/B Testing and Optimizing Your Email Campaigns

In the competitive world of email marketing for small businesses, it is crucial to not only create engaging and eye-catching email campaigns but also to continuously optimize them for maximum effectiveness. One of the most effective ways to achieve this is through A/B testing.

A/B testing, also known as split testing, involves creating two versions of your email campaign and sending them to a small sample of your audience. By testing different elements such as subject lines, call-to-action buttons, or images, you can gather valuable insights into what resonates best with your target audience.

Subject lines play a crucial role in determining whether your email gets opened or not. With A/B testing, you can test different subject lines to see which ones have higher open rates. For instance, you can try using a straightforward subject line in one version and a more creative and enticing subject line in the other. By analyzing the open rates of both versions, you can identify which subject line style works best for your audience.

Another element to test is the call-to-action (CTA) button. The placement, color, and wording of your CTA can significantly impact click-through rates. A/B testing allows you to experiment with different variations of your CTA to see which one generates the most clicks. For example, you can test a bold and colorful CTA button against a more subtle and minimalist design. By analyzing the click-through rates, you can optimize your CTA to drive better conversions.

Images are also powerful tools in email marketing. A/B testing can help you determine which images resonate better with your audience. You can test different visuals, such as product images, lifestyle images, or illustrations, to see which ones result in higher engagement. By understanding your audience's preferences, you can curate visually appealing email campaigns that capture their attention.

Furthermore, A/B testing can be used to optimize the timing and frequency of your email campaigns. By testing different send times and frequencies, you can identify the optimal schedule that generates the highest open and click-through rates. This way, you can ensure that your emails reach your audience at the most convenient and engaging times.

In conclusion, A/B testing is an essential tool for small business owners looking to optimize their email campaigns. By testing various elements such as subject lines, CTAs, images, and timing, you can gain valuable insights into what resonates best with your audience. Continuously experimenting and optimizing your email campaigns will help you achieve higher open rates, click-through rates, and ultimately drive better results for your small business.

Chapter 8: Analyzing and Measuring Email Marketing Success

Tracking Email Marketing Metrics

One of the most significant advantages of email marketing is the ability to track and analyze various metrics to measure the success of your campaigns. By monitoring these metrics, small business owners can gain valuable insights into the effectiveness of their email marketing efforts and make data-driven decisions to optimize their strategies. In this subchapter, we will explore the essential email marketing metrics that small business owners should track to enhance their campaigns and achieve their business goals.

1. Open Rate: The open rate indicates the percentage of recipients who opened your email. By analyzing this metric, you can determine the success of your subject lines and gauge the interest of your subscribers. A low open rate may indicate a need for improvement in your email content or targeting strategies.

2. Click-through Rate (CTR): The CTR measures the percentage of recipients who clicked on a link within your email. It provides insights into the relevancy and effectiveness of your email content and call-to-action. A high CTR indicates engaged subscribers, while a low CTR might signal a need for better content or stronger CTAs.

3. Conversion Rate: The conversion rate measures the percentage of recipients who took the desired action after clicking on a link in your email. This action could be making a purchase, signing up for a webinar, or downloading a resource. Tracking this metric helps you evaluate the effectiveness of your email campaigns in driving desired outcomes.

4. Bounce Rate: The bounce rate indicates the percentage of emails that were not successfully delivered to recipients. It can be categorized into two types: hard bounces (permanent delivery failures) and soft bounces (temporary delivery issues). By monitoring this metric, you can identify and resolve any deliverability problems, ensuring that your messages reach your intended audience.

5. Unsubscribe Rate: The unsubscribe rate reveals the percentage of subscribers who opted out of receiving your emails. It provides insights into the relevance and engagement of your content. A high unsubscribe rate may indicate a need for improvement in your email content or segmentation strategies.

6. ROI: Return on Investment (ROI) measures the profitability of your email marketing campaigns. By tracking the revenue generated from your email campaigns and comparing it to the costs incurred, you can determine the success and profitability of your efforts.

By regularly tracking and analyzing these email marketing metrics, small business owners can gain a deeper understanding of their audience, identify areas for improvement, and optimize their campaigns for better results. This data-driven approach will enable you to make informed decisions and continually refine your email marketing strategies to achieve your business objectives.

Analyzing Conversion Rates and ROI

As a small business owner, you understand the importance of email marketing in growing your business. However, it's not enough to simply send out emails and hope for the best. To truly harness the power of email marketing, you need to analyze your conversion rates and return on investment (ROI). In this subchapter, we will dive deep into the world of analyzing conversion rates and ROI to help you make data-driven decisions and optimize your email marketing campaigns.

Conversion rates are a vital metric that measures the percentage of recipients who take the desired action, such as making a purchase or signing up for a newsletter, after receiving your email. By analyzing conversion rates, you can identify what works and what doesn't in your email campaigns, allowing you to make targeted improvements. We will explore various strategies to track and monitor your conversion rates, including using tracking codes, setting up conversion goals, and utilizing analytics tools.

ROI, on the other hand, is a monetary measure of the profitability of your email marketing campaigns. It helps you determine the effectiveness of your investment in email marketing and whether it's generating a positive return. We will guide you through calculating ROI, considering both the costs associated with your email marketing efforts and the revenue generated as a result. Moreover, we will discuss ways to increase your ROI through effective segmentation, personalized content, and optimizing your email deliverability.

Throughout this subchapter, we will provide practical examples and case studies specific to small businesses. You will learn how to interpret your conversion rates and ROI data to identify areas of improvement and make informed decisions. We will also discuss key performance indicators (KPIs) that play a crucial role in evaluating the success of your email marketing campaigns.

By analyzing conversion rates and ROI, you will gain valuable insights into your email marketing strategy. This knowledge will empower you to refine your campaigns, enhance customer engagement, and ultimately drive more sales. Whether you are a small business owner looking to launch your first email marketing campaign or seeking to optimize your existing efforts, this subchapter will equip you with the tools and knowledge needed to succeed.

Remember, email marketing is not just about sending emails; it's about analyzing the results and using the data to continuously improve your approach. Get ready to dive into the world of conversion rates and ROI analysis and take your email marketing efforts to the next level!

Using Data to Improve Your Email Marketing Strategy

As a small business owner, you understand the importance of email marketing in reaching and engaging your target audience. However, simply sending out emails is not enough to guarantee success. To truly maximize the impact of your email campaigns, you need to leverage data to inform and improve your strategy. By analyzing key metrics and user behavior, you can gain valuable insights that will help you tailor your emails for better results.

One of the first steps in using data to enhance your email marketing strategy is to examine your open rates. This metric shows you the percentage of recipients who actually open the emails you send. By tracking open rates, you can identify patterns and trends to understand what subject lines, send times, or email designs resonate most with your audience. Experimenting with different variables and analyzing the corresponding data will allow you to optimize your emails for higher open rates.

Similarly, click-through rates (CTR) provide valuable information about the effectiveness of your email content. By measuring the percentage of recipients who click on links within your emails, you can gauge how engaging and compelling your calls-to-action are. Analyzing the CTR data will help you identify which types of content or offers resonate most with your audience, allowing you to refine your email content accordingly.

Another crucial aspect of data-driven email marketing is understanding your audience's behavior. By tracking metrics such as bounce rates, unsubscribes, and spam complaints, you can identify any issues that may be hindering your email deliverability. Additionally, analyzing user engagement metrics, such as time spent reading your emails or the number of conversions generated, will provide insights into the effectiveness of your email campaigns.

To gather this data effectively, it is essential to utilize email marketing tools that offer robust analytics and reporting features. These tools provide detailed insights into your email campaigns, allowing you to track and measure the metrics that matter most to your business.

By leveraging data to inform your email marketing strategy, you can make well-informed decisions that improve your overall results. Whether it's optimizing subject lines, refining content, or identifying areas for improvement, data-driven insights will help you continuously enhance your email campaigns. Remember, the success of your small business's email marketing efforts lies in understanding your audience and tailoring your approach based on data-driven insights.

Chapter 9: Ensuring Email Deliverability and Compliance

Understanding Email Deliverability Factors

In today's digital era, email marketing has become an essential tool for small businesses to connect with their customers. However, even with a well-executed email marketing strategy, your efforts may go in vain if your emails fail to reach the recipients' inbox. This is where email deliverability factors come into play.

Email deliverability refers to the ability of an email to successfully land in the intended recipient's inbox, rather than getting caught in spam filters or being blocked altogether. As a small business owner, it is crucial to understand the factors that influence email deliverability to ensure your messages reach your subscribers and have a higher chance of being read.

1. Sender Reputation: The reputation of your email sending domain and IP address plays a significant role in deliverability. Maintaining a good sender reputation involves avoiding spam traps, keeping complaint rates low, and regularly monitoring bounce rates.

2. Authentication: Implementing proper authentication protocols, such as SPF (Sender Policy Framework) and DKIM (DomainKeys Identified Mail), adds credibility to your emails. These protocols verify the integrity of your emails and help prevent them from being flagged as spam.

3. Content and Formatting: The content and formatting of your emails can impact deliverability. Avoid using excessive capitalization, spam trigger words, and misleading subject lines. Additionally, ensure that your emails are properly formatted, mobile-friendly, and have a clear call-to-action.

4. List Hygiene: Maintaining a clean and engaged email list is crucial for deliverability. Regularly remove inactive subscribers, correct invalid email addresses, and encourage recipients to whitelist your email address.

5. Engagement Metrics: Email service providers (ESPs) monitor recipient engagement metrics, such as open rates, click-through rates, and spam complaints. High engagement signals to ISPs that your emails are desired by recipients, improving deliverability.

6. ISP Relations: Building positive relationships with internet service providers (ISPs) can help improve deliverability. Monitor ISP-specific guidelines and best practices, establish feedback loops, and maintain open lines of communication with ISPs.

7. Deliverability Testing: Regularly test your emails using deliverability testing tools to identify potential issues before sending them to your subscribers. These tools assess your email against spam filters and provide valuable insights on deliverability.

By understanding and implementing these email deliverability factors, small business owners can significantly enhance the effectiveness of their email marketing campaigns. Remember, delivering your emails to the inbox is the first step towards engaging your audience, driving conversions, and ultimately growing your business.

Avoiding Spam Filters and Promotions Tabs

As a small business owner, you understand the importance of email marketing in reaching out to your target audience and driving sales. However, it can be frustrating to invest time and effort in crafting the perfect email campaign, only to have it end up in your customers' spam filters or promotions tabs, where it is likely to be overlooked or ignored. In this subchapter, we will explore effective strategies to help you avoid these obstacles and ensure that your emails land directly in your customers' primary inbox.

1. Build a High-Quality Email List: The first step in avoiding spam filters is to build a permission-based email list. Avoid purchasing email lists or adding contacts without their consent, as this can lead to high bounce rates and trigger spam filters. Instead, focus on growing your list organically by offering valuable content and incentives that encourage customers to subscribe.

2. Use Double Opt-In: Implement a double opt-in process to ensure that subscribers genuinely want to receive emails from your business. This method requires users to confirm their subscription by clicking on a verification link sent to their email address. This helps reduce the chances of fake or mistyped email addresses, improving the quality of your list.

3. Craft Engaging Subject Lines and Content: Spam filters often analyze the subject line and content of an email to determine its legitimacy. Avoid using

spam trigger words, excessive capitalization, or excessive exclamation marks in your subject lines. Additionally, personalize your content and make it relevant to your audience to increase engagement and reduce the likelihood of your emails being marked as spam.

4. Monitor Your Email Deliverability: Regularly check your email deliverability rates to identify any potential issues. Use email deliverability tools to track bounce rates, open rates, and spam complaints. If you notice a decline in deliverability, investigate the cause and take corrective actions promptly.

5. Segment Your Audience: Segmenting your email list based on customer preferences, demographics, or past purchase behavior allows you to send targeted and relevant content to specific groups. This increases engagement and reduces the chances of your emails being marked as spam.

6. Test and Optimize: Continuously test different elements of your emails, such as subject lines, sender names, and content format. Analyze the performance metrics and optimize your emails based on the results to improve deliverability and engagement.

By following these strategies, you can significantly reduce the chances of your emails ending up in spam filters or promotions tabs. Remember that building a strong relationship with your audience and providing value through your emails is crucial in ensuring your messages are well-received and acted upon.

Complying with Email Marketing Laws and Regulations

In today's digital age, email marketing has become an essential tool for small businesses to reach out and engage with their target audience. However, it is crucial for small business owners to be aware of and comply with email marketing laws and regulations to ensure the success and legality of their campaigns.

Email marketing laws and regulations are in place to protect consumers from spam, ensure privacy, and maintain the integrity of email communication. Non-compliance with these laws can have severe consequences, including hefty fines, damage to your brand reputation, and even legal action. Therefore, it is imperative to understand and adhere to the following key regulations:

1. CAN-SPAM Act: The CAN-SPAM Act sets guidelines for commercial email messages. It requires businesses to include accurate header information, provide a clear and conspicuous opt-out mechanism, and clearly identify the

message as an advertisement. Additionally, it prohibits the use of deceptive subject lines and mandates that businesses honor opt-out requests promptly.

2. General Data Protection Regulation (GDPR): If your business operates in the European Union or collects data from EU residents, you must comply with the GDPR. This regulation emphasizes transparency, consent, and control over personal data. It is essential to obtain explicit consent from subscribers, provide access to their data, and honor their right to be forgotten.

3. The Controlling the Assault of Non-Solicited Pornography and Marketing (CAN-SPAM) Act: Similar to the CAN-SPAM Act, the CASL aims to reduce the flow of spam and unwanted electronic messages. If your business targets Canadian customers, you must comply with CASL's requirements, which include obtaining consent, providing identification information, and offering an easy unsubscribe option.

4. California Consumer Privacy Act (CCPA): The CCPA grants California residents specific rights regarding their personal data. It requires businesses to disclose data collection practices, provide opt-out options, and secure personal information. Even if you are not based in California, complying with the CCPA can help build trust with your audience.

To ensure compliance with these laws and regulations, small business owners should implement the following best practices:

1. Obtain consent: Always seek explicit permission from subscribers before adding them to your email list. Use double opt-in methods to confirm their consent.

2. Provide clear identification and contact information: Include your business name, physical address, and a way for recipients to contact you in every email.

3. Offer easy opt-out options: Make it simple for subscribers to unsubscribe from your emails. Provide a visible and functional unsubscribe link in every communication.

4. Keep records: Maintain records of consent, opt-outs, and other relevant data to demonstrate your compliance with email marketing laws.

By understanding and complying with email marketing laws and regulations, small business owners can build trust with their subscribers, protect their brand reputation, and achieve long-term success in their email marketing efforts. Remember, being ethical and responsible in your email marketing practices will not only keep you on the right side of the law but also foster a positive relationship with your customers.

Chapter 10: Strategies for Growing Your Email List

Leveraging Social Media for List Growth

In today's digital age, social media has become an invaluable tool for small business owners looking to grow their email marketing lists. With millions of users actively engaged on platforms like Facebook, Instagram, and Twitter, the potential for reaching and connecting with new customers is immense. In this subchapter, we will explore effective strategies for leveraging social media to expand your email list and boost your small business's marketing efforts.

1. Create Compelling Content: To attract followers and encourage them to join your email list, it is crucial to consistently produce high-quality, engaging content. Share valuable information, tips, and industry insights that resonate with your target audience. By providing valuable content, you will establish yourself as an expert in your niche, enhancing your credibility and increasing the likelihood of users wanting to join your email list.

2. Implement Lead Magnets: A lead magnet is an incentive offered to potential subscribers in exchange for their email addresses. It can be a free e-book, a discount code, or exclusive access to educational resources. Promote your lead magnets on social media platforms to entice followers to sign up for your email list. Make sure the value of the lead magnet aligns with your target audience's interests and needs, increasing the chances of conversion.

3. Run Contests and Giveaways: Everyone loves the opportunity to win something. Running social media contests and giveaways is an excellent way to generate excitement and encourage users to join your email list. To participate, require entrants to provide their email address, allowing you to capture valuable leads. Ensure that the prize is relevant to your niche and appeals to your target audience to attract genuine subscribers.

4. Engage with Your Audience: Social media is all about building relationships and engaging with your audience. Respond to comments, messages, and mentions promptly and thoughtfully. By actively engaging with your followers, you not only foster a sense of community but also increase the chances

of them joining your email list. Encourage conversations, ask questions, and seek feedback to create a more interactive and personal experience.

5. Utilize Social Media Ads: Social media platforms offer powerful advertising tools that allow you to target specific demographics and reach potential customers who may be interested in your small business. Create compelling ads that highlight the benefits of joining your email list and target them to your ideal audience. Experiment with different ad formats and messaging to optimize your campaign's performance.

By leveraging the power of social media, small business owners can effectively grow their email marketing lists and expand their customer base. Implement these strategies to maximize your reach, engage with your audience, and ultimately, drive more conversions for your business.

Running Effective Email Marketing Campaigns

Email marketing has proven to be a powerful tool for small businesses to engage with their customers, drive sales, and build brand loyalty. By implementing effective email marketing campaigns, small business owners can maximize their reach and achieve significant results. In this subchapter, we will explore the key strategies and best practices to help small business owners optimize their email marketing efforts.

1. Building a Targeted Email List:

The success of an email marketing campaign starts with a well-segmented and targeted email list. Small business owners should focus on collecting email addresses from interested customers and prospects. This can be achieved through website sign-up forms, social media campaigns, or in-store promotions. By segmenting the list based on demographics, interests, or purchase history, businesses can send personalized and relevant emails that resonate with their audience.

2. Crafting Engaging Email Content:

Content is king in email marketing. Small business owners should aim to create compelling and valuable content that captures the attention of their subscribers. This can include informative newsletters, exclusive promotions, or useful tips and tricks. It is crucial to keep the content concise, visually appealing, and mobile-friendly to ensure optimal engagement.

3. Implementing Automation and Personalization:

Automation tools can streamline email marketing campaigns, saving time and effort for small business owners. By utilizing automation, businesses can send personalized emails triggered by specific actions or events, such as a welcome email for new subscribers or abandoned cart reminders. Personalization further enhances the effectiveness of email marketing, as customers feel valued and understood.

4. Testing and Analyzing Campaigns:

To ensure continuous improvement, small business owners should regularly test and analyze their email campaigns. A/B testing can help determine the most effective subject lines, call-to-action buttons, or email designs. By tracking key metrics such as open rates, click-through rates, and conversions, businesses can gain valuable insights and make data-driven decisions to optimize future campaigns.

5. Ensuring Compliance and Building Trust:

Small business owners must adhere to email marketing regulations, such as obtaining consent from subscribers and providing an easy unsubscribe option. Building trust is essential in email marketing, and businesses should focus on delivering relevant content, maintaining consistent branding, and respecting the privacy of their subscribers.

In conclusion, running effective email marketing campaigns is a crucial aspect of small business success. By building targeted email lists, crafting engaging content, utilizing automation and personalization, testing and analyzing campaigns, and ensuring compliance and trust, small business owners can harness the power of email marketing to drive growth, build customer relationships, and achieve their business goals.

Partnering with Influencers for List Building

In the realm of email marketing for small businesses, one highly effective strategy to rapidly build your subscriber list is by partnering with influencers. Influencers are individuals who have established credibility and a large following in a specific niche. Leveraging their influence can provide a significant boost to your list-building efforts and help you reach a wider audience.

So, how can small business owners effectively partner with influencers to grow their email lists? Here are some key steps to consider:

1. Identify Relevant Influencers: Begin by identifying influencers in your industry or niche who align with your brand values and target audience. Look for those who have a strong online presence, engage with their followers, and have a genuine interest in your products or services.

2. Build a Relationship: Once you have identified potential influencers, take the time to establish a relationship with them. Engage with their content, share it, and provide thoughtful comments. This will help you gain their attention and begin building rapport.

3. Offer Value: Influencers are often inundated with requests for collaborations. To stand out, offer something of value to them. It could be exclusive content, a special discount for their followers, or even a joint webinar or workshop. By providing value, you increase the likelihood of them agreeing to work with you.

4. Collaborate on Content: One effective way to leverage an influencer's reach is by collaborating on content. This could involve guest blogging, co-creating videos or podcasts, or even hosting joint webinars. By creating content together, you tap into their audience and expose your brand to a wider group of potential subscribers.

5. Create Irresistible Opt-ins: When partnering with influencers, it is crucial to have compelling opt-ins that resonate with their audience. Develop lead magnets or exclusive offers that align with the influencer's content and provide value to their followers. This will entice their audience to join your email list.

6. Promote Across Channels: Once you have created your irresistible opt-ins, work with the influencer to promote them across various channels. This could include social media shoutouts, dedicated emails, or even featuring your opt-ins in their blog posts. By leveraging the influencer's reach, you can quickly grow your subscriber list.

Partnering with influencers can be a game-changer for small business owners looking to expand their email marketing reach. By identifying the right influencers, building relationships, offering value, collaborating on content, creating irresistible opt-ins, and promoting across channels, you can effectively use influencers to build a highly engaged and responsive email list.

Chapter 11: Building Customer Relationships through Email Marketing

Using Email to Strengthen Customer Loyalty

As a small business owner, one of your primary goals is to build a loyal customer base. After all, loyal customers are more likely to make repeat purchases, refer your business to others, and provide valuable feedback. While there are various marketing strategies to achieve this, email marketing has emerged as a highly effective tool for small businesses to strengthen customer loyalty.

Email marketing allows you to establish a direct line of communication with your customers, enabling you to engage and connect with them on a personal level. By delivering targeted and relevant content right to their inbox, you can create a sense of exclusivity and make them feel valued. This personal touch is crucial in building trust and fostering long-term relationships.

To leverage email marketing effectively, it is essential to understand your audience and their needs. Segment your email list based on customer preferences, purchase history, or demographics, and tailor your messages accordingly. By sending personalized offers, recommendations, and updates, you can demonstrate that you understand your customers' interests and preferences, making them more likely to stay engaged and loyal.

Another powerful way to strengthen customer loyalty through email marketing is by offering exclusive discounts, promotions, or rewards. By making your customers feel special and appreciated, you not only encourage repeat purchases but also create a sense of urgency and excitement. Limited-time offers or VIP access can not only drive sales but also create a buzz around your brand, further enhancing customer loyalty.

Additionally, email marketing provides an opportunity to gather feedback and insights directly from your customers. Conduct surveys or request reviews to understand their experiences and expectations. Actively listening to your customers and implementing their feedback demonstrates that you value their opinions, leading to increased customer satisfaction and loyalty.

Remember, consistency is key in maintaining customer loyalty through email marketing. Design a well-planned email campaign that includes regular newsletters, product updates, and relevant content. By consistently providing value and staying top-of-mind, you can nurture customer relationships and encourage ongoing engagement.

In conclusion, email marketing is a powerful tool for small businesses to strengthen customer loyalty. By personalizing content, offering exclusive rewards, and actively listening to their needs, you can build trust, foster strong relationships, and create a loyal customer base that will support your business for years to come.

Implementing Customer Retention Strategies

In the world of small business, customer retention is crucial for long-term success. Acquiring new customers can be expensive and time-consuming, making it even more important to focus on nurturing and retaining the customers you already have. This subchapter will explore various customer retention strategies specifically tailored for small businesses in the realm of email marketing.

1. Personalized Communication: One of the most effective ways to retain customers is by personalizing your communication with them. Use email marketing tools to segment your customer base and send targeted messages based on their preferences, purchase history, and demographics. By making customers feel valued and understood, you can build strong relationships that encourage loyalty.

2. Offer Exclusive Benefits: Reward your existing customers by offering them exclusive benefits that are not available to new customers. This can include special discounts, freebies, or early access to new products or services. By making your customers feel special and appreciated, they are more likely to remain loyal and continue doing business with you.

3. Provide Exceptional Customer Service: Excellent customer service plays a significant role in customer retention. Make sure to promptly respond to customer inquiries and resolve any issues they may have. By going above and beyond to provide exceptional service, you can create a positive experience that encourages customers to stay loyal to your business.

4. Regularly Engage with Customers: Keep your customers engaged by regularly sending them valuable content, such as newsletters, blog posts, or industry updates. This will not only keep your business at the forefront of their

minds but also position you as an expert in your niche. By consistently providing value, you can build trust and loyalty among your customer base.

5. Request and Act on Customer Feedback: Encourage your customers to provide feedback on their experiences with your business. Actively listen to their suggestions and concerns, and make necessary improvements based on their feedback. By involving your customers in the decision-making process, you can show them that their opinions are valued, ultimately strengthening their loyalty.

In conclusion, customer retention is vital for the long-term success of small businesses. By implementing personalized communication, offering exclusive benefits, providing exceptional customer service, regularly engaging with customers, and acting on their feedback, you can create a customer-centric approach to email marketing. These strategies will not only help you retain your existing customers but also foster loyalty and increase customer lifetime value.

Utilizing Email for Upselling and Cross-Selling

In today's competitive business landscape, small business owners need to leverage every opportunity to maximize their revenue and grow their customer base. One effective strategy is to utilize email marketing for upselling and cross-selling. By leveraging the power of email, small businesses can not only increase sales but also enhance customer loyalty and satisfaction.

Upselling involves encouraging customers to upgrade their purchase by offering them a higher-priced item or a more advanced version of a product or service. Cross-selling, on the other hand, involves suggesting complementary products or services that can enhance the customer's experience or meet their additional needs. Both strategies can significantly boost a small business's bottom line.

Email marketing provides a cost-effective and personalized way to implement upselling and cross-selling strategies. By segmenting your email list based on customer preferences, past purchases, or demographics, you can tailor your offers to resonate with each recipient. Personalization is key to making your customers feel valued and increasing their likelihood of responding positively to your offers.

When crafting your upselling and cross-selling emails, it's crucial to focus on the benefits and value that your additional products or services can bring to the customer. Highlight how the upgrade or complementary item can enhance their experience, save them time, or solve a problem they may not have realized they had. By clearly communicating the value proposition, you can increase the chances of conversion.

To further enhance the effectiveness of your upselling and cross-selling emails, consider using persuasive language and creating a sense of urgency. Limited-time offers, exclusive discounts, or bonus incentives can create a sense of FOMO (Fear of Missing Out) and motivate customers to take immediate action.

However, it's important to strike a balance between promoting additional products and overwhelming your customers with too many offers. Bombarding your email list with constant upselling and cross-selling attempts can lead to unsubscribes and a negative brand image. Timing is crucial, so ensure that you space out your offers and provide valuable content in between.

In conclusion, utilizing email marketing for upselling and cross-selling is a powerful strategy for small business owners. By segmenting your email list, personalizing your offers, and effectively communicating the value proposition, you can increase sales and foster customer loyalty. Remember to strike a balance and provide valuable content to maintain a positive brand image. With the right approach, email marketing can be a game-changer for small businesses looking to thrive in today's competitive market.

Chapter 12: Advanced Email Marketing Techniques

Implementing Behavioral Triggers in Your Emails

In today's digital age, email marketing has become an essential tool for small businesses to reach and engage with their target audience. However, with inboxes flooded with numerous promotional emails, it can be challenging to stand out from the crowd and grab the attention of your recipients. This is where implementing behavioral triggers in your emails can make a significant impact on your email marketing efforts.

What are behavioral triggers, you ask? Well, they are actions or events that trigger specific email messages to be sent to your subscribers based on their behavior or interaction with your website or previous emails. By leveraging behavioral triggers, you can create highly personalized and timely emails that resonate with your audience, leading to increased engagement, conversions, and ultimately, more revenue for your small business.

One of the most common and effective behavioral triggers is the "abandoned cart" trigger. If a potential customer adds items to their shopping cart but fails to complete the purchase, an automated email can be triggered, reminding them of their abandoned cart and offering an incentive to encourage them to complete the transaction. This simple yet powerful trigger has been proven to recover lost sales and boost overall conversion rates.

Another valuable behavioral trigger is the "browse abandonment" trigger. If a subscriber visits your website, views specific products or services, but leaves without making a purchase, an automated email can be triggered, showcasing those products or offering additional information to entice them back. By reminding them of their interest and providing tailored recommendations, you can increase the chances of converting those leads into paying customers.

Furthermore, behavioral triggers can be used to re-engage inactive subscribers. By tracking their inactivity and sending personalized emails with exclusive offers, content, or invitations to events, you can reignite their interest and encourage them to re-engage with your brand.

To implement behavioral triggers effectively, you will need an email marketing platform that offers robust automation capabilities. These platforms allow you to set up and customize triggers based on specific actions or events, ensuring that the right message is delivered to the right person at the right time.

In conclusion, implementing behavioral triggers in your emails is a game-changer for small businesses looking to maximize the impact of their email marketing campaigns. By sending personalized, timely, and relevant messages to your subscribers based on their behavior and interaction with your brand, you can significantly improve engagement, conversions, and ultimately, drive more revenue for your small business. So, take the leap and start implementing behavioral triggers in your email marketing strategy today!

Personalizing Email Content Based on User Actions

In the world of email marketing for small businesses, one size does not fit all. Every customer is unique, and their actions can provide valuable insights into their preferences and interests. By personalizing email content based on user actions, small business owners can deliver targeted and relevant messages that resonate with their audience, leading to higher engagement and conversion rates.

Understanding user actions is crucial for effective personalization. By tracking and analyzing user interactions such as email opens, clicks, purchases, and website visits, small business owners can gain valuable data to tailor their email content. This data-driven approach allows them to segment their email list and deliver highly targeted messages to different customer segments.

Segmentation is the key to successful personalization. By dividing their email list into smaller groups based on user actions, small business owners can create more relevant content that caters to each segment's specific interests and needs. For example, customers who have made a recent purchase can be sent personalized product recommendations or exclusive discounts on related items. On the other hand, subscribers who have shown interest in a specific topic can receive curated content and resources related to that subject.

Personalization goes beyond simply addressing subscribers by their first names. It involves creating dynamic and customized content that adapts to the user's behavior and preferences. By integrating user data with their email marketing platform, small business owners can automate personalized email campaigns that respond to user actions in real-time. For instance, if a subscriber abandons their shopping cart, an automated email can be triggered to remind them of the items left behind and even offer a special discount to encourage them to complete the purchase.

The benefits of personalizing email content based on user actions are clear. It helps small business owners build stronger relationships with their audience, boosts customer engagement, and ultimately drives more sales. By leveraging user data and segmentation, small business owners can deliver targeted and relevant messages that resonate with their subscribers, making their email marketing campaigns more effective and efficient.

In conclusion, personalizing email content based on user actions is a powerful strategy for small business owners engaged in email marketing. By analyzing user interactions, segmenting their email list, and creating dynamic content, they can deliver tailored messages that captivate their audience and drive better results. With the right tools and approaches, personalization can take your email marketing to new heights, helping your small business thrive in today's competitive landscape.

Incorporating User-generated Content in Your Emails

In today's digital era, email marketing has become an essential tool for small businesses to reach and engage with their audience. But with inboxes flooded with promotional emails, how can you make your messages stand out? The answer lies in incorporating user-generated content (UGC) into your emails.

User-generated content refers to any form of content that is created by your customers or followers. It can be in the form of reviews, testimonials, social media posts, videos, or even blog articles. By leveraging UGC in your email marketing strategy, you can not only boost engagement but also build trust and credibility with your target audience.

One of the most effective ways to incorporate UGC in your emails is by featuring customer reviews or testimonials. By showcasing positive feedback from satisfied customers, you can provide social proof and encourage others to trust and try your products or services. Including a short snippet of a customer's positive review in your email can be a powerful tool to entice recipients to take action.

Another great way to integrate UGC is by featuring user-generated images or videos. If your customers have shared pictures or videos of themselves using your products or services on social media, why not include them in your emails? Not only does this add authenticity to your brand, but it also creates a sense of community and encourages others to share their experiences.

In addition to reviews and images, you can also incorporate UGC by highlighting user-generated blog articles or social media posts that mention your brand. This not only provides valuable content for your emails but also helps to foster relationships with your customers. By acknowledging and sharing their content, you show that you value their opinions and contributions.

When incorporating UGC in your emails, make sure to obtain permission from the creators and give proper credit. This not only protects your brand's reputation but also ensures that you are complying with copyright laws.

In conclusion, incorporating user-generated content in your emails is a valuable strategy for small businesses. By leveraging the positive experiences and opinions of your customers, you can build trust, boost engagement, and ultimately drive conversions. So, start tapping into the power of UGC and watch your email marketing efforts soar to new heights!

Chapter 13: Integrating Email Marketing with Other Marketing Channels

Combining Email Marketing with Social Media

In today's digital age, small businesses are constantly seeking innovative ways to reach their target audience and build a strong online presence. While email marketing has long been recognized as an effective strategy, the integration of social media platforms can take your small business to new heights. In this subchapter, we will discuss the power of combining email marketing with social media and how it can benefit small business owners.

Social media platforms, such as Facebook, Instagram, Twitter, and LinkedIn, have become an integral part of people's daily lives. By leveraging these platforms alongside your email marketing efforts, you can amplify your brand's visibility and engage with a wider audience. Here's why this combination is essential for small businesses:

1. Expanding your reach: Social media allows you to connect with a vast network of potential customers, enabling you to expand your reach beyond your email subscriber list. By posting engaging content, sharing promotions, and interacting with your followers, you can attract new leads and convert them into loyal customers.

2. Building brand loyalty: Social media gives your small business a personality and allows you to build a community around your brand. By sharing valuable content, responding to comments, and fostering conversations, you can establish trust and loyalty among your audience, ultimately driving customer retention.

3. Driving traffic to your website: By incorporating social media links in your email marketing campaigns, you can direct your subscribers to your website or specific landing pages. This synergy enhances the chances of conversions and boosts your website's traffic, leading to increased sales and revenue.

4. Cross-promotion opportunities: Social media and email marketing can work hand in hand to promote each other. Encourage your email subscribers to follow your social media profiles and vice versa. By leveraging both platforms,

you can create a cohesive marketing strategy that reinforces your brand's message and maximizes exposure.

5. Enhanced customer insights: By monitoring social media engagement, you can gain valuable insights into your audience's preferences, interests, and behaviors. Use this information to personalize your email campaigns, ensuring that you deliver the right message to the right audience at the right time.

In conclusion, combining email marketing with social media is a powerful strategy that small business owners should embrace. It allows you to expand your reach, build brand loyalty, drive traffic to your website, cross-promote effectively, and gain valuable customer insights. By implementing an integrated marketing approach, you can take your small business to new heights and achieve sustainable growth in today's competitive digital landscape.

Syncing Email Marketing with Content Marketing

In today's digital age, small businesses are constantly seeking effective strategies to reach and engage with their target audience. Two powerful approaches that have proven to be game-changers for small businesses are email marketing and content marketing. While both tactics can be highly effective on their own, they become even more powerful when synced together. This subchapter explores the synergy between email marketing and content marketing and how small businesses can leverage this union to maximize their marketing efforts.

Email marketing is a direct and personalized way to communicate with your audience. By using email campaigns, small businesses can send tailored messages to their subscribers, nurturing relationships, and driving conversions. On the other hand, content marketing focuses on creating valuable and relevant content to attract and engage potential customers. This content can take various forms, such as blog posts, videos, infographics, or podcasts, and is designed to educate, entertain, or inspire the target audience.

The key to syncing email marketing with content marketing lies in using email campaigns to distribute and amplify content. By incorporating links to your latest blog posts, videos, or other content in your email newsletters, you can drive traffic to your website or blog. This not only increases the visibility of your content but also nurtures your subscribers by providing them with valuable information.

Furthermore, syncing these two strategies allows you to repurpose your content for email campaigns. Instead of creating separate content for your emails, you can repurpose existing blog posts or videos by adapting them into a format suitable for email newsletters. This saves time and effort while ensuring consistent messaging across different channels.

To make the most out of this synergy, it's essential to align your email marketing and content marketing goals. Understanding your target audience's preferences, interests, and pain points will help you create content that resonates with them. By analyzing email campaign metrics such as open rates, click-through rates, and conversions, you can gain insights into the type of content that drives engagement and conversions.

In conclusion, syncing email marketing with content marketing is a winning strategy for small businesses. By integrating these two tactics, you can amplify your content reach, nurture your subscribers, and drive conversions. This subchapter has explored the benefits and strategies behind this powerful union, providing small business owners with the tools they need to master their email and content marketing efforts.

Leveraging Email in Multichannel Marketing Campaigns

In today's fast-paced digital landscape, it is crucial for small businesses to implement effective multichannel marketing campaigns in order to reach and engage with their target audience. One of the most powerful tools at their disposal is email marketing. In this subchapter, we will explore how small business owners can leverage email in their multichannel marketing campaigns to maximize their reach, engagement, and ultimately, their business growth.

Email marketing has long been regarded as a cost-effective and efficient way to communicate with customers. With its high ROI and ability to deliver personalized and targeted messages, email has become a staple in the marketing toolbox of small businesses. However, to truly harness its potential, it is essential to integrate email marketing into a broader multichannel strategy.

The first step in leveraging email in multichannel marketing campaigns is to understand your target audience and their preferences. By collecting data and insights from various channels, such as social media and website analytics, small business owners can gain valuable insights into their customers' behaviors, preferences, and purchase patterns. Armed with this information, they can create highly targeted and relevant email campaigns that resonate with their audience.

Another key aspect of leveraging email in multichannel marketing campaigns is to ensure consistency across all channels. Small business owners should strive to create a seamless and integrated experience for their customers, whether they are interacting with the brand through email, social media, or in-store. By aligning the messaging, branding, and offers across all channels, businesses can reinforce their brand identity and build trust with their customers.

Additionally, small business owners should explore the power of automation and personalization in their email campaigns. By leveraging automation tools, they can send timely and relevant emails based on customer actions or preferences, such as abandoned cart reminders or personalized product recommendations. This level of personalization not only enhances the customer experience but also increases the likelihood of conversions and repeat purchases.

Lastly, it is crucial for small business owners to track and analyze the performance of their email campaigns. By monitoring key metrics, such as open rates, click-through rates, and conversion rates, businesses can identify areas for improvement and optimize their campaigns for better results. This data-driven approach allows small business owners to make informed decisions and continuously refine their multichannel marketing strategies.

In conclusion, email marketing plays a pivotal role in the success of small businesses' multichannel marketing campaigns. By leveraging the power of email, small business owners can reach their target audience, deliver personalized messages, and drive engagement and conversions. However, it is important to integrate email marketing into a broader multichannel strategy, ensuring consistency, automation, personalization, and data-driven optimization. By doing so, small business owners can unlock the true potential of email in their marketing efforts and achieve sustainable business growth.

Chapter 14: Overcoming Email Marketing Challenges

Dealing with Email Deliverability Issues

As a small business owner, email marketing can be a powerful tool to establish and grow your brand. It allows you to connect with your customers directly, build relationships, and drive conversions. However, one of the most common challenges faced by small businesses in email marketing is deliverability issues. In this subchapter, we will discuss the common problems associated with email deliverability and provide effective strategies to overcome them.

1. Understanding Email Deliverability:

Email deliverability refers to the ability of your emails to reach the recipient's inbox successfully. It involves various factors such as sender reputation, email content, spam filters, and recipient engagement. Understanding these factors is crucial to ensuring your emails are delivered and read by your target audience.

2. Identifying Deliverability Issues:

To address deliverability issues, you first need to identify them. We will discuss common problems like high bounce rates, low open rates, or landing in spam folders. By monitoring your email metrics and using email deliverability tools, you can pinpoint the issues and take appropriate actions.

3. Building a Solid Sender Reputation:

Your sender reputation plays a vital role in email deliverability. We will guide you on how to maintain a positive reputation by following best practices, such as using a reputable email service provider, authenticating your domain, and implementing proper email list hygiene.

4. Crafting Engaging and Relevant Content:

Email content that resonates with your audience is more likely to be opened and engaged with. We will provide tips on creating personalized, valuable, and visually appealing content that encourages recipients to interact with your emails, reducing the chances of being flagged as spam.

5. Complying with Anti-Spam Laws:

Understanding and adhering to anti-spam laws is essential to avoid deliverability issues. We will highlight key legislation, such as the CAN-SPAM

Act and GDPR, and guide you on how to obtain consent, include necessary opt-out options, and maintain email compliance.

6. Testing and Optimizing:

To improve email deliverability, continuous testing and optimization are crucial. We will discuss different techniques, including A/B testing subject lines, sender names, and email designs, as well as analyzing email deliverability reports to identify areas for improvement.

By implementing the strategies outlined in this subchapter, you can effectively tackle email deliverability issues and improve the success of your small business email marketing campaigns. Remember, building a strong sender reputation, creating engaging content, following anti-spam laws, and constantly optimizing your email strategy are key steps towards mastering email marketing for small businesses.

Handling Unsubscribes and Bounce Rates

In the world of email marketing for small businesses, handling unsubscribes and bounce rates is a crucial aspect that cannot be ignored. Unsubscribes and bounce rates are inevitable and are a part of any email marketing campaign, regardless of its size or industry. However, understanding how to effectively manage these aspects can make a significant difference in the success of your email marketing efforts.

Unsubscribes occur when recipients choose to opt-out of receiving further emails from your business. While it may be disheartening to see subscribers leave, it is essential to respect their decision. To handle unsubscribes effectively, it is recommended to provide a clear and easy-to-find unsubscribe link in every email. By doing so, you not only comply with email marketing regulations but also demonstrate your commitment to respecting your subscribers' preferences. Additionally, consider including a feedback option for those who choose to unsubscribe, allowing them to provide valuable insights that can help you improve your future email campaigns.

Bounce rates, on the other hand, occur when an email fails to reach its intended recipient's inbox. Bounces can be either hard or soft. Hard bounces indicate permanent delivery failures, such as an invalid or non-existent email address, while soft bounces are temporary and often caused by issues like a full inbox or a temporary server problem. It is crucial to regularly monitor and analyze bounce rates to identify any underlying issues with your email list quality or technical aspects of your email marketing platform. Regular list cleaning and maintenance, as well as using double opt-ins, can significantly help minimize bounce rates.

To effectively handle both unsubscribes and bounce rates, it is essential to maintain a healthy and engaged email list. Continuously monitor the engagement metrics of your emails, such as open rates and click-through rates, to identify subscribers who may be disengaged or uninterested. Consider segmenting your email list based on engagement levels and tailor your content and offers accordingly. By providing relevant and valuable content to your subscribers, you can increase their engagement and decrease the chances of them unsubscribing or bouncing.

In conclusion, handling unsubscribes and bounce rates is an integral part of email marketing for small businesses. By implementing best practices such as providing clear unsubscribe options, monitoring bounce rates, maintaining a healthy email list, and delivering engaging content, you can effectively manage these aspects and optimize the success of your email marketing campaigns. Remember, building strong relationships with your subscribers is key, and respecting their preferences and maintaining high deliverability rates will contribute to your overall email marketing mastery.

Troubleshooting Common Email Marketing Problems

Email marketing has become an indispensable tool for small businesses to reach out to their customers and drive sales. However, like any other marketing strategy, it is not without its challenges. In this subchapter, we will explore some of the most common email marketing problems faced by small business owners and provide practical solutions to overcome them.

1. Low Open Rates: One of the most frustrating issues is when your emails go unnoticed. To overcome this problem, focus on crafting captivating subject lines that pique the recipient's curiosity. Additionally, segment your email list based on customer preferences and behavior to ensure targeted and relevant content.

2. High Unsubscribe Rates: Losing subscribers can be disheartening, but it is essential to understand why people are unsubscribing. Review your email content

and frequency to ensure you are providing value without overwhelming your audience. Consider offering incentives or exclusive deals to encourage subscribers to stay engaged.

3. Landing in Spam Folders: Deliverability issues can significantly impact the success of your email marketing campaigns. To avoid being marked as spam, regularly check your sender reputation, ensure you have permission-based lists, and optimize your email content to avoid triggers that flag spam filters.

4. Poor Click-through Rates: If your subscribers are not clicking on your links, it's time to reassess your call-to-action (CTA) strategy. Make your CTAs clear, concise, and visually appealing to entice readers to take action. Consider using enticing visuals, personalized offers, or limited-time promotions to increase click-through rates.

5. Inconsistent Branding: Maintaining a consistent brand image is crucial for building trust and recognition. Ensure your email templates, design elements, and tone of voice align with your overall brand identity. Consistency across all touchpoints, including social media and website, enhances brand loyalty and recognition.

6. Lack of Personalization: Generic emails are often ignored, so personalization is key. Leverage customer data to personalize subject lines, content, and offers. Use dynamic fields to address subscribers by name and segment your lists to send targeted messages based on preferences, purchase history, or demographics.

7. Technical Issues: Email marketing platforms may occasionally encounter technical glitches that affect the delivery or tracking of emails. Stay updated with platform updates and promptly report any issues to their support teams for resolution.

By understanding and proactively addressing these common email marketing problems, small business owners can optimize their campaigns and achieve better results. Remember, email marketing is an ongoing process that requires experimentation, data analysis, and continuous improvement to achieve long-term success in engaging and converting customers.

Chapter 15: Best Practices for Email Marketing Success

Staying Up-to-Date with Email Marketing Trends

In today's digital age, email marketing has emerged as one of the most effective and cost-efficient ways for small businesses to reach their target audience. However, with the ever-evolving landscape of technology and consumer behavior, it is essential for small business owners to stay up-to-date with the latest email marketing trends. This subchapter aims to provide small business owners with valuable insights and practical tips on how to keep their email marketing strategies relevant and impactful.

One of the key aspects of staying up-to-date with email marketing trends is understanding the changing preferences and behaviors of your target audience. Consumer expectations are constantly evolving, and what worked in the past may not be effective anymore. By conducting regular market research and analyzing customer data, small business owners can gain valuable insights into their customers' preferences, allowing them to tailor their email marketing campaigns accordingly.

Another important trend in email marketing is the rise of mobile devices. With the majority of consumers accessing their emails through smartphones and tablets, it is crucial for small business owners to optimize their email campaigns for mobile devices. This includes using responsive email templates, ensuring that the content is easily readable on smaller screens, and optimizing loading times for mobile users.

Personalization is another key trend that small business owners should prioritize in their email marketing efforts. Generic, one-size-fits-all emails are no longer effective in capturing the attention of consumers. By segmenting their email lists based on demographics, preferences, or purchase history, small business owners can deliver personalized and relevant content that resonates with their target audience. This can lead to higher open rates, click-through rates, and ultimately, better conversion rates.

In addition to these trends, small business owners should also keep an eye on emerging technologies and innovations in the email marketing industry. From artificial intelligence and machine learning to interactive emails and personalized video content, staying informed about these advancements can give small business owners a competitive edge and help them stand out in a crowded inbox.

In conclusion, staying up-to-date with email marketing trends is crucial for small business owners looking to maximize the impact of their email campaigns. By understanding their target audience, optimizing for mobile devices, personalizing content, and embracing emerging technologies, small business owners can ensure that their email marketing strategies remain relevant, engaging, and effective in today's ever-changing digital landscape.

Engaging in Continuous Testing and Optimization

In the fast-paced digital world, staying ahead of the curve is crucial for small business owners looking to maximize the benefits of email marketing. As a small business owner, you understand that email marketing is a powerful tool that can help you connect with your target audience, boost conversions, and ultimately grow your business. However, to truly master this marketing strategy, you must engage in continuous testing and optimization.

Continuous testing involves regularly experimenting with different elements of your email campaigns to determine what resonates best with your audience. By testing various aspects such as subject lines, content, layout, and call-to-action buttons, you can gain invaluable insights into what works and what doesn't. This data-driven approach allows you to make informed decisions and refine your email marketing strategy over time.

One of the key benefits of continuous testing is the ability to optimize your email campaigns for maximum effectiveness. Optimization involves making incremental improvements based on the insights gained from testing. For example, if you discover that a certain subject line generates higher open rates, you can incorporate similar language and tactics into future campaigns. Similarly, if you find that a specific call-to-action button drives more clicks, you can replicate its design and placement in subsequent emails.

Engaging in continuous testing and optimization also helps you stay relevant and adapt to changes in consumer behavior. By monitoring key metrics like open rates, click-through rates, and conversion rates, you can identify trends and adjust your strategies accordingly. For instance, if you notice a decline in open rates on mobile devices, it may be time to optimize your emails for mobile responsiveness.

Additionally, continuous testing and optimization allow you to personalize your email marketing efforts. By segmenting your audience based on demographics, purchase history, or engagement level, you can tailor your messages to their specific needs and preferences. Personalization not only increases the likelihood of conversions but also helps build stronger relationships with your customers.

In conclusion, as a small business owner, embracing continuous testing and optimization is essential for mastering email marketing. By constantly experimenting, analyzing data, and making incremental improvements, you can refine your strategies, increase engagement, and drive conversions. Remember, the digital landscape is ever-evolving, and staying ahead requires a proactive approach to testing and optimization.

Building Long-term Relationships through Email Marketing

In today's digital age, email marketing has emerged as a powerful tool for small businesses to connect with their customers and build long-lasting relationships. With its cost-effectiveness and high return on investment, email marketing has become an essential strategy for businesses of all sizes. This subchapter aims to provide small business owners with a hands-on approach to mastering email marketing and leveraging it to cultivate strong, long-term relationships with their customers.

One of the key benefits of email marketing is its ability to personalize communication with customers. By collecting valuable data on customer preferences, purchasing habits, and interests, small businesses can tailor their email campaigns to resonate with their target audience. Personalization not only enhances the customer experience but also fosters a sense of loyalty and trust, ultimately strengthening the long-term relationship between the business and its customers.

Another essential aspect of building long-term relationships through email marketing is delivering relevant and valuable content to subscribers. Small businesses should focus on creating engaging and informative content that adds value to their customers' lives. This can include product updates, industry news, helpful tips, and exclusive offers. By consistently delivering valuable content, businesses can position themselves as trusted authorities in their niche and keep customers engaged and interested in their brand.

Segmentation is a crucial strategy for small businesses looking to build long-term relationships through email marketing. By dividing their email list into different segments based on demographics, interests, or purchase history, businesses can send highly targeted and relevant content to each group. This ensures that customers receive emails that are tailored to their specific needs and interests, leading to higher engagement and conversion rates.

Furthermore, small businesses should focus on nurturing their email subscribers by implementing automated email sequences. These sequences can include welcome emails, onboarding series, and re-engagement campaigns. By automating these processes, businesses can consistently engage with their customers, even when they are not actively present, and nurture the relationship over time.

Lastly, monitoring and analyzing email marketing metrics is essential for small businesses to optimize their campaigns and improve their long-term relationship-building efforts. Metrics such as open rates, click-through rates, and conversion rates provide valuable insights into the effectiveness of email campaigns. By analyzing these metrics, businesses can identify areas for improvement and make data-driven decisions to enhance their email marketing strategies.

In conclusion, email marketing provides small businesses with a powerful tool to build long-term relationships with their customers. By personalizing communication, delivering valuable content, segmenting their email list, nurturing subscribers, and analyzing metrics, small businesses can leverage email marketing to foster loyalty, trust, and engagement, ultimately driving long-term success.

Conclusion: Your Email Marketing Journey Begins Here

As a small business owner, you understand the importance of reaching out to your customers and building strong relationships with them. Email marketing has emerged as one of the most effective strategies for achieving this goal. In this book, "Email Marketing Mastery: A Hands-On Approach for Small Business Owners," we have explored the world of email marketing and provided you with the necessary tools and knowledge to embark on your own successful email marketing journey.

Throughout this book, we have delved into the various aspects of email marketing for small businesses, offering practical advice and actionable steps that you can implement right away. We have discussed the importance of building a quality email list, crafting compelling and engaging email content, and optimizing your email campaigns for maximum impact.

Now that you have reached the end of this book, it is time to put your newfound knowledge into action. Your email marketing journey begins here. Take the time to reflect on what you have learned and consider how you can apply it to your own business.

First and foremost, start by building a strong foundation for your email marketing efforts. Focus on growing your email list organically, ensuring that you only have subscribers who are genuinely interested in what you have to offer. Implement best practices for collecting email addresses, such as offering valuable content in exchange for sign-ups, and make it easy for visitors to subscribe to your emails on your website and social media platforms.

Once you have a solid email list, it is time to create compelling content that will engage your subscribers. Craft personalized and targeted emails that resonate with your audience, addressing their pain points and providing solutions. Experiment with different types of content, such as newsletters, product updates, and promotional offers, to keep your subscribers interested and coming back for more.

In addition to content creation, it is crucial to monitor and optimize your email campaigns. Track key metrics such as open rates, click-through rates, and conversions to gauge the success of your campaigns. Use this data to refine your strategies and continuously improve your email marketing efforts.

Remember, email marketing is an ongoing process that requires consistent effort and adaptation. Stay up to date with the latest trends and best practices in the industry, and continue to experiment and innovate with your email campaigns. By staying committed and dedicated to your email marketing journey, you will be able to build lasting relationships with your customers and drive growth for your small business.

So, take the knowledge you have gained from this book, put it into practice, and watch your email marketing efforts flourish. Your success starts now. Good luck on your email marketing journey!

Don't miss out!

Visit the website below and you can sign up to receive emails whenever Tyler Ryan publishes a new book. There's no charge and no obligation.

https://books2read.com/r/B-A-LLJAB-CKVNC

BOOKS 2 READ

Connecting independent readers to independent writers.

www.ingramcontent.com/pod-product-compliance
Lightning Source LLC
Chambersburg PA
CBHW050606160726
48003CB00003B/1068